Yosemite
NATIONAL PARK

Long before it was integrated into the National Park Service in 1916, Yosemite was designated by President Abraham Lincoln on June 30, 1864, as an inalienable public trust. This was the first action by any government in the world that set aside land for the enjoyment of its citizens. Influential people were involved very early in Yosemite's modern history including Galen Clark, who became the first guardian of the Yosemite Grant at President Lincoln's signing of the Yosemite Valley Grant Act. John Muir was also involved in Yosemite's history, convincing Theodore Roosevelt to sign a bill that placed control of the Valley and the Mariposa Grove with the federal government in 1906. Today, Yosemite stands as one of the crown jewels of America's National Parks.

Tuolumne Meadows

Yosemite's high country is dotted with Lodgepole Pine, Western White Pine, and Whitebark Pine trees. These grow between the ponds, pools, lakes and granite domes. This area is very popular for camping and hiking.

30 miles from Yosemite Valley, on Tioga Road, sits White Wolf Lodge. 30 miles beyond White Wolf Lodge is Tuolumne Meadows Lodge. Also located in the high country are tent cabin camps that are accessible on foot or horseback. All three are excellent locations for hikers and backpackers with trail access nearby leading to beautiful vistas and peaks throughout Yosemite's high country.

Snow can be found in the higher elevations of the park nearly year-round. When it does melt, it forms ponds, streams and adds to the lakes already in the area. The snowmelt in this area feeds water to Yosemite Falls, Horsetail Fall, and others throughout the park.

Tenaya Lake

The mighty Merced River guides us into Yosemite Valley as we enter from the west.

The first waterfall one sees upon entering Yosemite Valley is graceful Bridalveil Fall. The primary source of Bridalveil Fall is Ostrander Lake which is over 10 miles to the south.

Bridalveil Fall
620 feet (189m)

El Capitan
3,593 feet (1095m) above valley floor

El Capitan is one of the most recognizable features of Yosemite National Park and is a mecca for climbers. The first time The Nose was climbed was in 1958 by Warren J. Harding, Wayne Merry and George Whitmore.

El Capitan soars more than 3,000 feet above the valley floor. The granite formations of Yosemite were formed between 80 and 200 million years ago.

Valley View

This is one of the few easily accessible locations in the park where visitors can see El Capitan, the Merced River and Bridalveil Fall at the same time. For that reason, this is a very popular spot to take pictures at any time of the year.

Visitors to the park enjoy rafting and canoeing on the Merced River as it wanders through Yosemite Valley. From early Spring to late summer, water levels are sufficient for these popular water activities.

Sentinel Rock
7,038 feet (2,145m)

Cathedral Rocks and Spires form the eastern side of the canyon through which Bridalveil Creek flows and can be viewed on the south valley wall to the east of Bridalveil Fall. Its overall elevation is 6014 ft (1833m).

This series of three successive peaks lies east of El Capitan on the north side of Yosemite Valley. From top to bottom, they are Eagle Peak, Middle Brother and Lower Brother. The elevation of Eagle Peak, the tallest of the three, is 6,713 ft (2,046 m).

Yosemite Chapel is one of the few chapels inside a national park, though it no longer sits at its original site at the base of Four Mile Trail. It was moved to its present location in the fall of 1901 to be nearer to the hotels, businesses and other community activities in the valley at the time.

Yosemite Falls
2,425 feet (739m)

Spectacular Yosemite Falls measures a stunning 2,425 foot (739m) drop from top to bottom which includes the upper and lower sections of 1,430 feet (425m) and 320 feet (97m) respectively. The remaining 675 foot drop occurs in what are referred to as "the cascades". Yosemite Creek reforms at the base of Lower Yosemite Falls and quickly merges with the Merced River, which then flows out of the valley.

Lodging in Yosemite Valley is in high demand and is booked, in some cases, up to 12 months in advance.
Yosemite Lodge now occupies the space where Fort Yosemite, headquarters for the U.S. Army Cavalry in Yosemite, stood from 1906 until 1914.

The majestic Ahwahnee Hotel has been declared a National Historic Landmark and received that designation on May 28, 1987. It has 99 hotel rooms, parlors and suites as well as 24 cottage rooms. The rustic and elegant hotel, designed by architect Gilbert Stanley Underwood, was completed in 1927.

Curry Village, or Camp Curry, was founded in 1899 by a married couple from Indiana, David and Jennie Curry, both school teachers.

Black Bear *(Ursus americanus)*
Yosemite National Park is home to an estimated 300 - 500 black bears where they are relatively averse to human contact. Unlike the grizzly bear, black bears desire no contact with humans, even when defending their young.

The hike up Half Dome is very popular during the summer months when the number of hikers can easily surpass 1,000. It has been the subject of many books and photos. Half Dome is certainly one of the most recognizable features of Yosemite National Park, as well as being one of the most popular strenuous hikes.

Half Dome was thought to be completely inaccessible as late as the 1870's. However, today there are numerous ways to make it to the top. Most hikers take the 17-mile round trip, with the last portion of the climb assisted by steel cables which act as handrails.

In many respects, Half Dome is representative of Yosemite National Park. This massive granite monolith is famous worldwide because of its unique shape and descriptive name.

The Mist Trail leads hikers up to the top of Vernal Fall, but not before walking through the mist it produces. Starting at the Happy Isles trailhead, hikers walk a total of 1.3 miles (2km) to view it.

Vernal Falls
317 feet (97m)

Nevada Falls
594 feet (181m)

Access to Nevada Fall is 3.4 miles from the trailhead at Happy Isles in the valley. Hikers pass by Vernal Fall on their way in to see Nevada Fall, which lies 2 miles farther down the trail.

Yosemite National Park is home to a wide variety of plants, and each one adds to the majesty of the park.

With habitats that range from thick foothill chaparral to expanses of alpine rock, the park supports many species of mammals, reptiles, birds and insects.

Tunnel View offers an easily accessible location to view El Capitan, Bridalveil Fall and Half Dome all at the same time.

Tunnel View

With 104 rooms nestled in southern Yosemite, the Wawona Hotel has been in operation for nearly 130 years. Soon after it was completed in 1879, it became a premier location for travelers to stay while visiting the nearby Mariposa Grove and, of course, Yosemite Valley.

This historic bridge spans the South Fork of the Merced River at the south end of Yosemite in Wawona, near the Pioneer Yosemite History Center. The original structure was not covered and was built in 1868 by Galen Clark, the first steward of the "Yosemite Grant".

The Mariposa Grove Museum is inside of a cabin which was built in 1930 and restored in 1983. It occupies the site where Galen Clark built a small cabin in 1861.

In Mariposa Grove visitors will find the largest stand of sequoia trees in Yosemite National Park.

Badger Pass
7,200 feet (2,194 m)

This 90 acre (.36 sq. km2) skiing area provides 10 runs and 5 lifts with downhill, snow tubing and snowboarding facilities.
Badger Pass has served as a popular entry point to Yosemite's snow-covered back country for over 75 years. Cross-country skiing to Glacier Point is a perennial favorite of the resort's visitors.

Mt. Hoffmann *10,850 feet*

Polly Dome *9,790 feet*

Mirror Lake *4,098 feet*

Tresidder Peak *10,600 feet*

Echo Peaks *10,745 feet*

Clouds Rest *9,926 feet*

Half Dome *8,842 feet*

Glacier Point
7,214 feet (2,199m)

Mt. Broderick 6,696 feet
Grizzly Peak 6,056 feet
Mt. Maclure 12,693 feet
Mt. Florence 12,520 feet
Mt. Lyell 13,114 feet
Liberty Cap 7,057 feet
Vernal Fall 317 feet
Nevada Fall 594 feet
Mt. Clark 11,522 feet

Half Dome
As viewed from Glacier Point